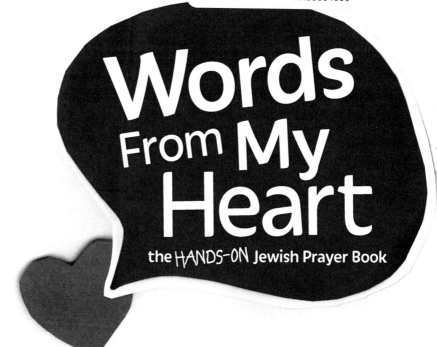

the HANDS-ON Jewish Prayer Book

Published by: Goldfinger

Text and Illustrations: Evelyn Goldfinger

Cover & Interior layout: Federico Pallas

Design consultant: Karen Feldman

With the support of ROI Community

ISBN: 978-1-7335165-7-0

Printed in the United States of America
First edition, 2022

www.shalomeve.com

With gratitude in my heart to the One who created the world with words; to the ones who came before us and handed the words to us; and to you, dear reader, who will carry the words forward. E.G.

In Loving Memory of my Bobe Chola Ana Roimiser Z"L.

Thank you to my dear friend Karen Feldman for your insights, for listening from your heart, and for helping in transforming my ideas into a visual reality. Thank you to my husband Federico Pallas for your support and love today and always, for your graphic expertise, and for challenging me to grow as an artist. Thank you to my son Jonathan for being my inspiration and for praying with me. Thank you to my parents and my sisters for their love always and for starting me in the journey of Jewish prayers and traditions. Thank you to my Bobe Chola Ana Roimiser Z"L for modeling the values of family and faith in G*d with such inner strength, yet in a humble way. Thank you to Joy Schandler for believing in my Words From My Heart approach and book since its early days. Thank you for your support, guidance, expertise, and friendship.

Thank you to my friends, colleagues, teachers, and fans for your reviews from your heart and for your support, including: Tanya Wisoker, Melisa Goldfinger, Lapiduz family, Leora Lazarus, Rosenthal family, Sandra Lilienthal, Atach family, Batsheva Frankel, Nina Gelman-Gans, Jennifer Zunikoff, Lisa Baydush, and Evonne Marzouk. A special thank you to my amazing launch team.

Table of Contents

Words for adults

We are soulful beings. Research shows that children are born with an innate spiritual disposition[1]. Just as we nurture children's bodies, minds, and emotions, we can give children the opportunity to practice and grow their spiritual dimension. *Words From My Heart, the hands-on Jewish Prayer Book* invites children to experience their spirituality through prayer, at their level.

Prayer is a practice. Just like working out strengthens our muscles, prayer requires training, guidance, and proper tools. When we pray, we awaken to an awareness of self, of oneness, of transcendence. We feel a connection to something greater.

Jewish prayer offers a framework for expressing our spirituality. Ritual gives us structure. However, our sages warn us not to make prayer fixed, but to act with intention[2]. In Judaism, we are invited to use our own words when we pray. This is known as *T'fillat HaLev*, the prayer from one's heart[3]. We usually tell children: "Use your words." Let's invite them to use their own words when they pray.

How to use this book

Words From My Heart, the hands-on Jewish Prayer Book is based on my family's practice and my work as an educator and spiritual leader. It also emerged from a song I wrote about four of the central concepts in Jewish prayer: *Todah* (thank you/gratitude), *B'vakashah* (please/asking for help), *S'lichah* (saying sorry/repairing our mistakes), and *Halleluyah* (exclaiming praise and awe). You can find the lyrics and the link to this song at the end of the book.

There are four sections in this book, each focusing on one of the prayer concepts noted above. Each chapter includes:

- Activities that invite children to explore the prayer concept in their own personal way through imagining, drawing, writing, cutting, and pasting.
- A Jewish prayer that connects to the prayer concept.
- Key words in Hebrew, noted with transliteration, translation, and Hebrew letters.

- An opportunity for children to write or draw their own prayer with the words from their hearts.
- Prayer sources meant for adults.
- A song and prayer video with Ms. Eve, a list of additional prayers, and more resources (through a QR code).

This book is not meant to be completed in one sitting. You may focus on one section at a time, or you may choose to delve into each concept with one of its corresponding activities. I invite you to guide your child or students by reading the prompts out loud to them or with them. Explore the book together.

The word G*d is written in this way to invite you to name the Divine[4] in a way that works for you. Some possibilities are God, *Adonai*[5], *Hashem*, Source, One, Force of Nature, Divine Feminine, *Sh'chinah* (Divine Feminine Presence), Higher Power, or Spirit of Life.

Whether you are exploring this prayer book at home or with your students at school, encourage children to say or express the words that live in their hearts. They can also bring this book to the synagogue or to other soulful gatherings.

With gratitude in my heart (*Lev*) to you, dear reader, and to the One who created the world with words,

Evelyn "Ms. Eve" Goldfinger

---

1. I recommend reading the research on the subject by Dr. Lisa Miller in *The Spiritual Child* and *The Awakened Brain*.

2. Our sages warn us not to make prayer (*T'fillah*) fixed (*Keva*), but to act with intention (*Kavanah*). See Pirkei Avot 2:13.

3. In the *Tanach* (Hebrew Bible) we can find numerous examples of spontaneous prayer. One example is Hannah. "Now Hannah, she spoke in her heart" (Samuel I 1:13).

4. Within the Hebrew Bible and Jewish prayers, G*d has different names. To make sure G*d's name is treated with respect, many Jewish traditions don't write the word G*d or certain other names for the Divine in full.

5. This book contains sacred words and written names for G*d. Please treat it with respect.

3

Shalom, chaverim! Hi, friends! I am so happy to share with you *Words From My Heart, the hands-on Jewish Prayer Book.*

The words in your heart (Lev - לֵב) are very important. You can use them to talk to others, to yourself, and even to G*d, the Creator of the world. When we talk with G*d, we call it prayer. We have many ways to say "G*d". When you see the word G*d in this book, you can read it in different ways, such as "God", "*Adonai*", "*Hashem*", "Spirit of Life", or "One". I like to think of G*d as "The Greatest Artist". I believe this world is a work of art and we are part of that art, with the gift to create wonderful things ourselves.

Jewish prayer is called T'fi**lah** (תְּפִלָה). People pray to talk to G*d and also to look inside themselves and to listen with their hearts.

There are many ways to pray: with others or by ourselves; at home, at the synagogue, or out in nature; in Hebrew or in our daily language. We can sing out loud, whisper, or just breathe. Sometimes we use a prayer book called Si**ddur** (סִדוּר), which has great words that people wrote many years ago.

Words From my Heart, the hands-on Jewish Prayer Book will help you use your own words in prayer. Please, make this book your own! You can draw on it, make notes, and play games with it. You can even write or draw your own prayers. I hope that you can use this prayer book to discover and to pray with the words that come from your heart.

With love,

Ms. Eve

4

Watch a story that inspires us to pray with the words in our hearts

This is me! *Draw or paste a picture of yourself.*

I - Ani - אֲנִי

My name is:

_____

5

Todah - תּוֹדָה
Thank you, G*d.

There is so much to say thank you for! You can say it out loud or think it in your head.

Thank you for the **PEOPLE** that I love, like...

Thank you for the **PLACES** that make me happy, like...

Thank you for the **ACTIVITIES** I enjoy doing, like...

Thank you for my favorite **THINGS**, like...

When I say **"THANK YOU, G*d"**, I can feel how lucky and blessed I am to have all these people, creatures, places, activities, and things in my life.

What do you want to say **TODAH** for?

House - **Ba**yit - בַּיִת

Look around and find:

 My favorite <u>toy</u>
(tza'a**tzu**a - צַעֲצוּעַ)

 My favorite <u>color</u>
(**tze**va - צֶבַע)

 Something that
I love playing with

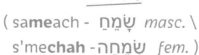 Something that
makes me <u>happy</u>
(sa**me**ach - שָׂמֵחַ *masc.* \
s'me**chah** - שְׂמֵחָה *fem.*)

 Someone I love

 A <u>picture</u> that
makes me smile
(t'mu**nah** - תְּמוּנָה)

 Something I can share

 A <u>mirror</u> (and smile
back at myself!)
(mar**'e** - מַרְאֶה)

 Something I want
to say "<u>Thank you</u>"
for today.
(to**dah** - תּוֹדָה)

7

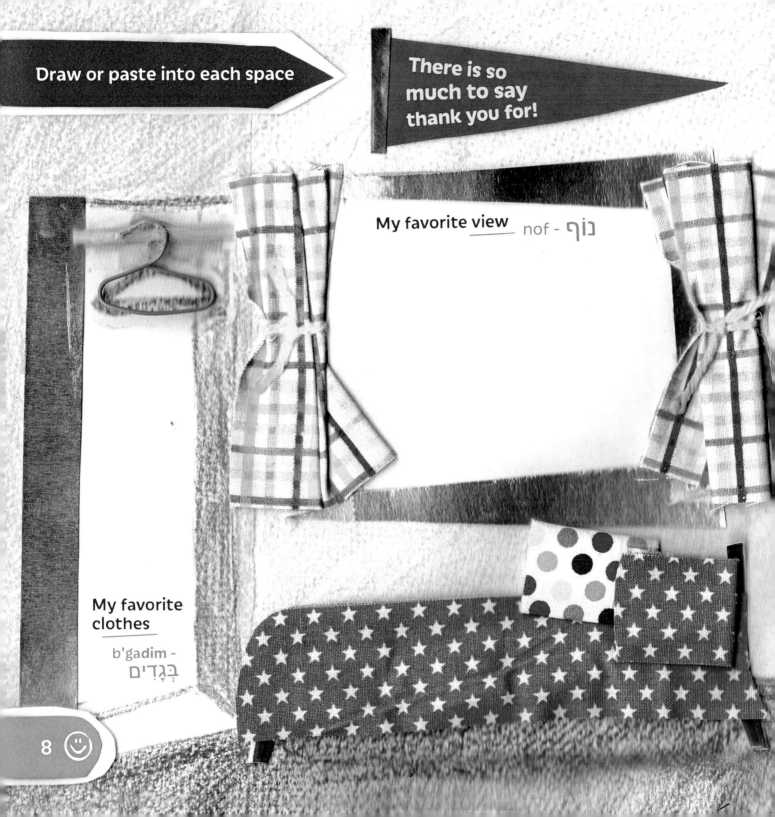

Draw or paste into each space

There is so much to say thank you for!

My favorite view ___ nof - נוֹף

My favorite clothes
___
b'gadim - בְּגָדִים

8 ☺

My favorite books
s'far**im** - סְפָרִים

My favorite moment

S	M	T	W	T	F	S

My favorite toy tza'a**tzu**'a - צַעֲצוּעַ

My favorite game
mis**chak** - מִשְׂחָק

My family   mishpa**chah** - מִשְׁפָּחָה

My...

My pet

ch**a**yat mach**mad**
חַיַת מַחְמָד

My favorite food
ochel - אֹכֶל

Draw or paste into each space

MODEH ANI
Morning Prayer of Thanks

מוֹדֶה אֲנִי לְפָנֶיךָ
מֶלֶךְ חַי וְקַיָּם
שֶׁהֶחֱזַרְתָּ בִּי
נִשְׁמָתִי בְּחֶמְלָה,
רַבָּה אֱמוּנָתֶךָ.

> The first thing that I say when I wake up is Modeh Ani. I give thanks to you, G*d, for returning my soul and for giving me the chance to enjoy another day. Thank you, G*d, for believing in me so much! I will do my best. I will take good care of myself, the people around me, and your world. I will enjoy this day!

Modeh* **ani** lefa**ne**cha
Melech chai veka**yam**,
Sheheche**zar**ta bi
nishmati b'**chem**lah,
Ra**bbah** emuna**te**cha!

* Girls and women say "Mo**dah**"(מוֹדָה).
  You can also say "O**deh**" (אוֹדֶה)
  in future tense, for all genders.

Thank you, G*d of life,
for placing my soul
in me with love;
You believe in me so much!

About this prayer
These words are from the prayer book (*Siddur*). This prayer first appeared in the work Seder HaYom by the 16th century Rabbi Moshe ben Machir. It's a great way to start one's day, with an attitude of gratitude and by being reminded that G*d cares for us and gives us the gift of a brand new day.

Watch and listen to Todah songs and prayers

Prayer means to speak to G*d. You can start with "Thank you, G*d, for..." or "Todah, G*d, I feel so happy when..." or "How lucky I am to..."

Todah - תּוֹדָה
Thank you, G*d.

B'vakashah - בְּבַקָשָׁה
Please, G*d.

S'lichah - סְלִיחָה
I am sorry, G*d.

Halleluyah - הַלְלוּיָה
Wow, G*d.

13

B'vaka**shah** - בְּבַקָשָׁה
Please, G*d.

What do you want to say **B'VAKASHAH** for?

_____

_____

_____

_____

Sometimes we want to ask for something.

And there are times when we need to ask for help. Did you know that we all need help sometimes? We can ask for help with small things and even with big challenges. We ask nicely by saying please (B'VAKA**SHAH** - בְּבַקָשָׁה).

We can ask other people for help, like our parents or teachers.

We can also ask G*d for help.

14

Argaz Keilim (אַרְגַּז כֵּלִים)

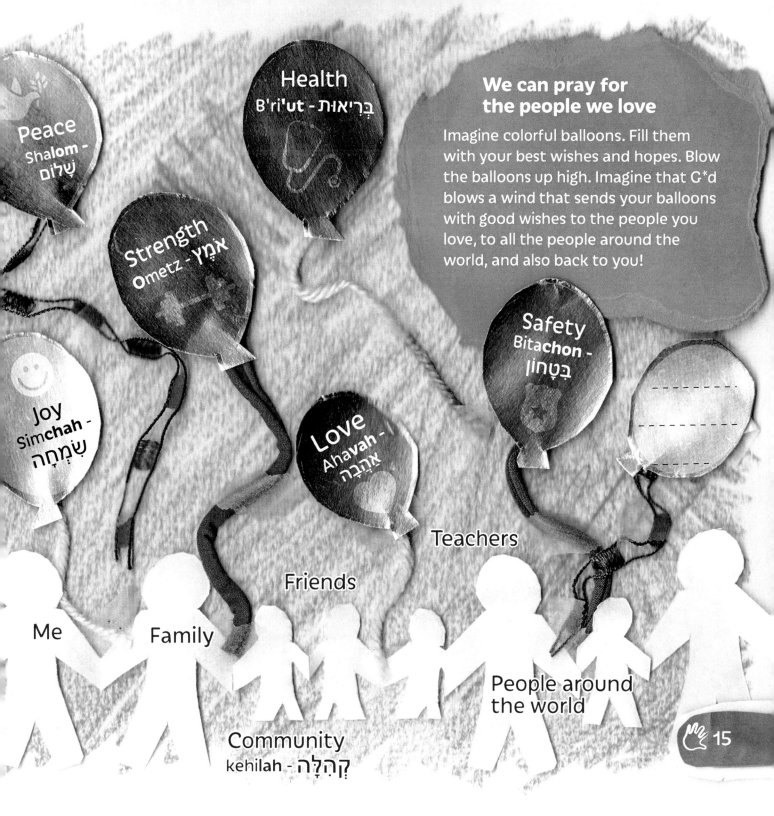

Peace
Shalom - שָׁלוֹם

Health
B'ri'ut - בְּרִיאוּת

Strength
Ometz - אֹמֶץ

We can pray for the people we love

Imagine colorful balloons. Fill them with your best wishes and hopes. Blow the balloons up high. Imagine that G*d blows a wind that sends your balloons with good wishes to the people you love, to all the people around the world, and also back to you!

Joy
Simchah - שִׂמְחָה

Love
Ahavah - אַהֲבָה

Safety
Bitachon - בְּטָחוֹן

Teachers

Friends

Me

Family

People around the world

Community
kehilah - קְהִלָּה

15

What do you need a helping hand with today?

Moving or changing schools

Making new friends

Trace your hand here.
Yad - יָד

For a friend to feel better!

Making better choices

Who can you ask for help?

16

Cut and give away

You can help too! Give a hand to someone you wish to help.

I will help by cleaning up!

I will give you a hug

I will listen and pay attention

How can I help you?

I will write a "get well" card

I will call to say "hi"

I will share with you

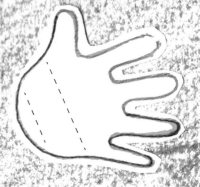

Cut and give away

Draw on this side what you can help with.

You can also write the name of the person you are giving a hand to.

Word Search

Can you find these words?

- **HELP** ✓
  ezrah - עֶזְרָה
- **HEART**
- **FRIEND**
- **FAMILY**
- **HAND**
- **GOD**
- **TOGETHER**
  b'yachad - בְּיַחַד
- **HUG**
  chibuk - חִבּוּק
- **PLEASE**
- **HEAL**
- **LAUGH**
  tz'chok - צְחוֹק
- **SMILE**
  chiyuch - חִיּוּךְ
- **LOVE**
  ahavah - אַהֲבָה

Q	U	H	E	L	P	A	N	J	O	L	G
U	L	U	I	S	A	B	O	B	E	T	O
T	R	G	L	C	E	N	R	S	I	O	P
F	A	M	I	L	Y	K	A	C	H	R	I
E	W	U	D	O	V	I	B	H	E	A	L
D	I	N	A	V	O	T	S	U	A	H	E
E	F	P	L	E	A	S	E	N	R	T	A
N	B	A	K	O	M	V	O	T	R	E	
H	O	M	U	F	R	I	E	N	D	O	N
A	R	Z	G	I	R	L	O	L	J	N	Q
N	I	M	H	A	Y	E	T	W	I	T	Y
D	U	T	O	G	E	T	H	E	R	Z	A
				L	I	V	E	H			

What do you need help with today? Can you find the first letter of that word in this word search?
milah - מִלָּה

19

EL NA R'FA NA LAH
Prayer for Healing

אֶל נָא רְפָא נָא לָה

Our words and actions are important. When we pray for someone to get better, we are sending out love and energy to them. It's a great Mitzvah (מִצְוָה) and a good thing to visit people who are not feeling well, calling them, making them a "get well soon" card, or helping them with their grocery shopping. Just knowing that you are thinking of them can make someone feel better!

El na r'**fa** na lah*.

* When praying for healing of a boy or men, we may say "R'**fa** na loh". We can also ask for our healing: "R'**fa** na **la**nu" (heal us) or "R'**fa** na li" (heal me).

Please, G*d,
help them
feel better.
Please!

About this prayer

These are the words that Moses uses when asking G*d to cure his sister Miriam (Numbers 12:13). It is short and easy to say, to remember, and/or to sing. Requests and needs are part of our prayers. The *Bakashot*, supplications, come from the same Hebrew root as the word B'vakashah. By acknowledging and expressing our needs and wants we reach out not only to G*d, but to our consciousness. We become aware. And that is an important step when seeking for help in times of need.

Watch and listen to B'vakashah songs and prayers

20

Prayer is when we have a talk with G*d. You can start with "Please, G*d, help me with..." or "B'vaka**shah**, G*d, how do I...?" Or "Dear G*d, give me strength to..." It can be just a few words as "guide me" or "be with me".

Todah - תּוֹדָה
Thank you, G*d.

B'vakashah - בְּבַקָּשָׁה
Please, G*d.

S'lichah - סְלִיחָה
I am sorry, G*d.

Halleluyah - הַלְלוּיָהּ
Wow, G*d.

21

S'lichah - סְלִיחָה
I am sorry, G*d.

What do you want to say **S'LICHAH** for?

When we know we made a mistake, we can start by saying "I am sorry" (**S'LICHAH** - סְלִיחָה). Sometimes we need to practice saying sorry because it may feel like a big word and we may feel shy to use it. But saying sorry is the first step to fixing our mistakes. It shows that we want to make it better. You can tell a person that you didn't mean to hurt them and that you want to make things right. You can even bring a toy or something nice to share with them.

We all make mistakes.

And we can all learn and practice how to make better choices.

Path - Derech - דֶּרֶךְ

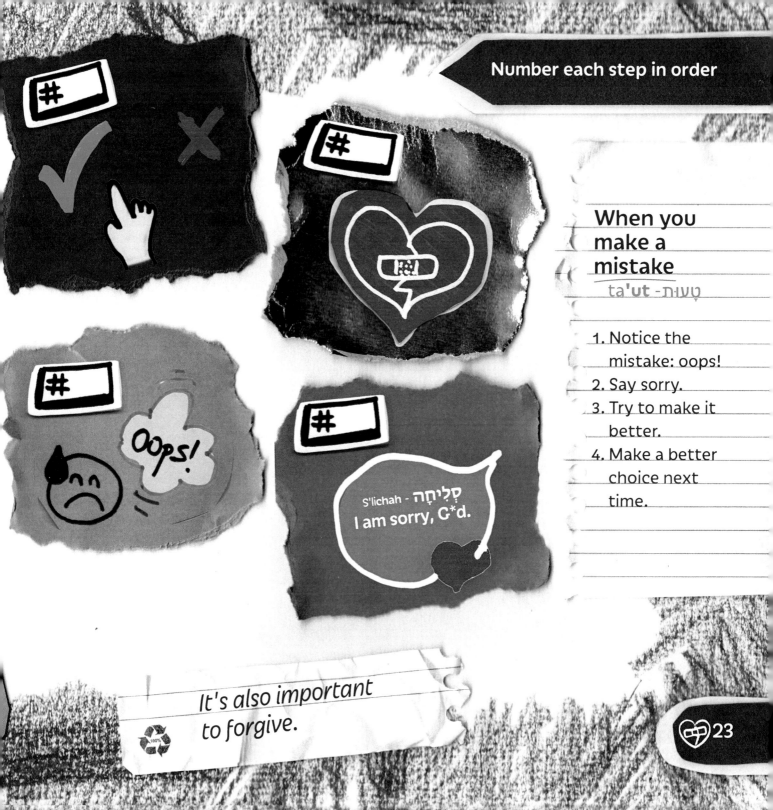

When you
make a
mistake
ta'ut - טָעוּת

1. Notice the
   mistake: oops!
2. Say sorry.
3. Try to make it
   better.
4. Make a better
   choice next
   time.

S'lichah - סְלִיחָה
I am sorry, G*d.

oops!

It's also important
to forgive.

23

We all make mistakes.

Can you think of one of your "oops" moments? What did you learn? How can you make it better next time?

Cut and give away

Write your s'lichah message on each heart.

To :
From:
I'm sorry for:

Oops!

I made a mistake!

Oy! Give me another chance!

Uh oh!

To :
From:
I'm sorry for:

Oops!

I will make it better by...

I am truly sorry.

I am happy we are friends again!

I forgive you!

Please, forgive me!

Cut and give away

Draw or write on this side how to make things better.

Maze Find one of the ways to patch the broken heart

Why do you think there is more than one way to solve this maze? Can you find more than one way to fix your mistakes? How about finding different reasons for forgiving?

27

S'LICHAH
Prayer for Saying I am Sorry

וְעַל כֻּלָּם אֱלוֹהַּ סְלִיחוֹת.
סְלַח לָנוּ. מְחַל לָנוּ. כַּפֶּר לָנוּ.

**Ve'al kulam
Eloha slichot.
Slach lanu. Mechal
lanu. Kaper lanu.**

For all our mistakes,
we say sorry,
forgiving G*d.

Forgive us.

Give us another
chance.

Help us make better
choices.

There are 4 steps to fixing our mistakes. When we take these steps, we call it "doing T'shuvah (תְּשׁוּבָה)".
1. Notice that you made a mistake. Oops!
2. Say sorry to the person you hurt, even if it was by accident.
3. Try to repair and to make it better.
4. Next time, make a better choice. That's when we learn from our mistakes!

About this prayer
These are the words we say on *Yom Kippur*, the Day of Atonement when we ask G*d for forgiveness. We find this prayer in the *Machzor*, the prayer book for the High Holidays. But we also recite a prayer for repentance every day in the *Amidah* (a central prayer in our daily prayer services). You can share with your child that *T'shuvah* (from the verb "to return") actually means more than saying sorry. It includes recognizing our mistakes, repairing, asking for forgiveness, and deciding to make better choices next time. Each day we have the opportunity to make things better. You can also talk with your child about the importance of forgiving others and ourselves.

Watch and listen to S'lichah
songs and prayers

28

Prayer is looking inside your heart. What are the words you want to share with G*d? It can be as simple as saying "I am sorry" or "I now know I didn't make a good choice when...", or "G*d, help me learn from this mistake and to make a better choice next time".

Write in your own words or draw a prayer for saying I'm sorry or asking for forgiveness.

Todah - תּוֹדָה
Thank you, G*d.

B'vakashah - בְּבַקָשָׁה
Please, G*d.

Halleluyah - הַלְלוּיָה
Wow, G*d.

S'lichah - סְלִיחָה
I am sorry, G*d.

Halleluyah - הַלְלוּיָהּ
Wow, G*d.

What do you want to say HALLELUYAH for?

How wonderful is G*d's world (olam - עוֹלָם)! And I get to be a part of it. This world is so special. I want to say "wow!" "HALLELU**YAH** (הַלְלוּיָהּ)" and enjoy all these awesome views, places, beings, and things that G*d created: nature, foods, plants, planets, adventures, animals, and people!

I was created by G*d, and my body, my mind, and my soul are very special.

All the different people I meet are special too.

1 thing I TASTE...
How does it taste?
Sweet or sour?
Salty?
Do you like this taste?
ta'am - טַעַם

2 things I SMELL...
How do they smell?
Is it a strong smell?
Is it sweet?
Do I like this smell?
reyach - רֵיחַ

3 things I TOUCH... How do they feel? Soft? Sharp? Hard? Wet? Hot? Cold?
Touch
maga - מַגָע

4 things I HEAR...
Are these sounds loud or soft? High pitch or low pitch? Fast or slow? Is it musical?
Sound
tz'lil - צְלִיל

5 things I SEE... Are they big or small? Near or far? Do I like them? What is their shape? What is their color?
Sight
re'yia - רְאִיָה

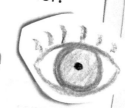

1 thing I FEEL... Do I like this feeling? If yes, how can I enjoy it? If not, can I talk about it with someone? Who can help me to deal with this feeling?
Feeling
regesh - רֶגֶש

31

Olam - עוֹלָם

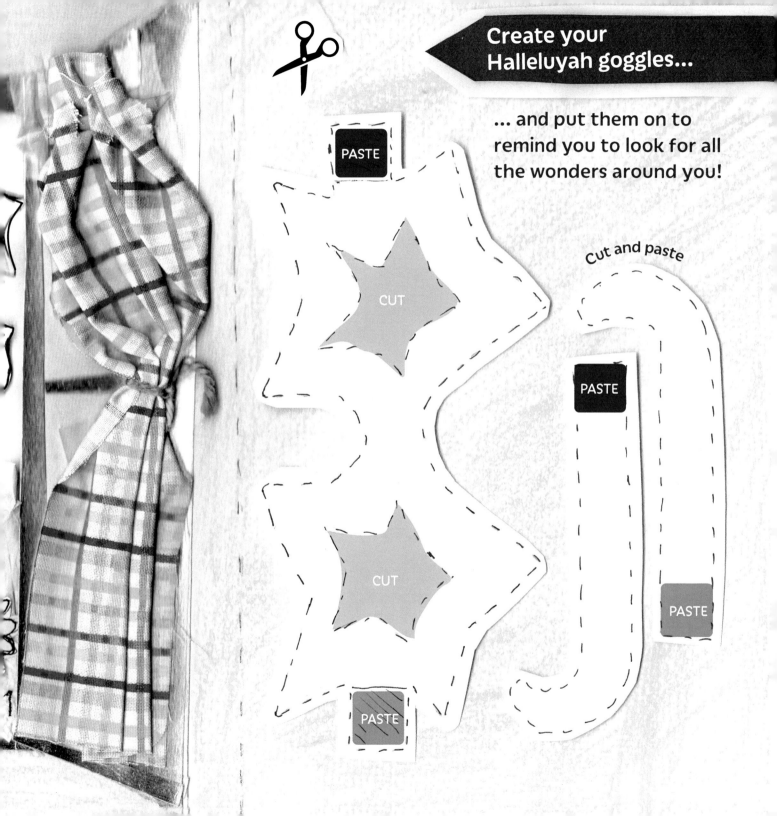

Create your Halleluyah goggles...

... and put them on to remind you to look for all the wonders around you!

PASTE

CUT

CUT

PASTE

Cut and paste

PASTE

PASTE

Find the wonders of the world!

(Back!)

Wonderful things to find...

1 Rainbow
keshet - קֶשֶׁת

1 Halleluyah Goggles
mishkafayim - מִשְׁקָפַיִם

6 Apples
tapuchim - תַּפּוּחִים

5 Butterflies
parparim - פַּרְפָּרִים

2 Balls
kadurim - כַּדּוּרִים

3 Stars
kochavim - כּוֹכָבִים

4 Bunnies
sh'fanim - שְׁפַנִּים

1 Heart
lev - לֵב

1 Hand
yad - יָד

When you go out today, pay close attention. Can you find something special?

meyuchad - מְיֻחָד

Can you name three things about it? Share what you found with your family or friends.

Put on your
Halleluyah goggles

HALLELUYAH!
Prayer of Praise

הַלְלוּהוּ בְּתֹף וּמָחוֹל
הַלְלוּהוּ בְּמִנִּים וְעֻגָב
הַלְלוּהוּ בְצִלְצְלֵי־שָׁמַע
הַלְלוּהוּ בְּצִלְצְלֵי תְרוּעָה
כֹּל הַנְּשָׁמָה תְּהַלֵּל יָהּ
הַלְלוּ־יָהּ

Hallelu**hu** b'**tof** uma**chol**,
Halleluhu b'mi**nim** v'u**gav**,
Halleluhu b'tziltz'**lei** sha**ma**,
Halleluhu b'tziltz'**lei** t'ru'**ah**.
Kol han'sha**mah** t'ha**llel** Yah
Halleluyah.

How amazing is G*d! We look around and we know that a very special, smart, powerful, loving, and imaginative Force created the universe. The sky and the sun, the sea and the trees, the little bees and the big whales, the roaring lions, and all the people. And how wonderful it is that we can to talk to G*d. We say "wow!" and we sing Halleluyah! (I sometimes even say "HalleluYAY!"). Saying "Halleluyah" is a prayer in itself. Sing it from your heart anytime you discover something amazing! How about singing along with your musical instruments?

Sing Halleluyah to G*d with tambourines and dance; Halleluyah with instruments of wind and strings; Halleluyah with percussion instruments; soft and loud. All creatures, let's say to G*d with a deep breath: Halleluyah!

About this prayer
Halleluyah is a Hebrew word that means "praise G*d." You can praise by repeating the word "Halleluyah." There are many Halleluyahs in the Psalms, *Tehilim*. These words are from Psalm 150.

Watch and listen to Halleluyah songs and prayers

When you pray you become a pray-er. Can you pray with your voice, your smile, or with your hands? Can you pray with a jump of joy or with a happy dance?

B'vakashah - בְּבַקָשָׁה
Please, G*d.

Todah - תּוֹדָה
Thank you, G*d.

S'lichah - סְלִיחָה
I am sorry, G*d.

Halleluyah - הַלְלוּיָה
Wow, G*d.

SH'MA ISRAEL
Prayer for Listening

שְׁמַע יִשְׂרָאֵל
יְיָ אֱלֹהֵינוּ
יְיָ אֶחָד

Sh'**ma** Isra**el**,
Ado**nai** Elo**hei**nu,
Ado**nai** E**chad**.

Listen, Israel:
Adonai is our G*d,
Adonai is ONE.

LISTEN sh'ma (שְׁמַע) to the special words in your heart. When saying the "Sh'ma Israel" (also often written "Shema Yisrael"), some people close their eyes to pay even more attention. Others try to listen with their hearts. When we say that G*d is the Higher Power, we recognize that we are part of something bigger than ourselves. G*d is one, and we are all part of THE ONE. And we are partners with G*d in taking good care of the people, animals, plants, places, and things in this world. We were all created by G*d, and so we are all special to G*d.

Watch and listen to the Sh'ma songs and prayers

About this prayer

The Sh'ma Israel is a central prayer of the Jewish faith. It is from the Hebrew Bible (*Tanach* - תָּנָ"ךְ). We can find it in Deuteronomy (*D'varim*) 6:4. The next paragraphs of the Sh'ma can be found in Deuteronomy (*D'varim*) 6:5–9, 11:13– 21, and Numbers (*Bemidbar*) 15:37–41. Known also as the "Shema," we proclaim out loud that *Adonai* is our G*d and that *Adonai* is ONE. We recognize the Divine, something greater than ourselves. We recite the "Shema" daily in our prayer services and also before going to sleep.

 Watch and listen to the song

Todah, B'vakashah, S'lichah, Halleluyah
a Words From My Heart song
by Evelyn "Ms. Eve" Goldfinger

שִׁיר - shir

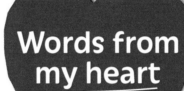

Words from my heart

לֵב - lev

Todah! Thank you!
תּוֹדָה

Todah for my *mishpachah* (my family),

Todah for my *chaverim* (my friends),

For my home, my toys, for all the good things,

Thank you, G*d, I say *Todah*.

Bevakashah! Please! בְּבַקָּשָׁה

B'vakashah guide me in my way,

B'vakashah make the ouches go away,

B'vakashah bring *Shalom* (peace) every day.

I ask you, please G*d, *B'vakashah*.

Slichah! Sorry!
סְלִיחָה

S'lichah for the mistakes I made,

S'lichah for the rude things I said,

For not listening when asked to behave (oops!)

I'm sorry, G*d, forgive me, *S'lichah*.

Halleluyah!
הַלְלוּיָה

Halleluyah! For the sky, the land, the sea,

Halleluyah! For the animals and the trees,

For the love I feel inside of me,

Wow, G*d, I say *Halleluyah!*

Todah, B'vakashah, S'lichah, Halleluyah!

תּוֹדָה , בְּבַקָּשָׁה, סְלִיחָה, הַלְלוּיָה !

 39

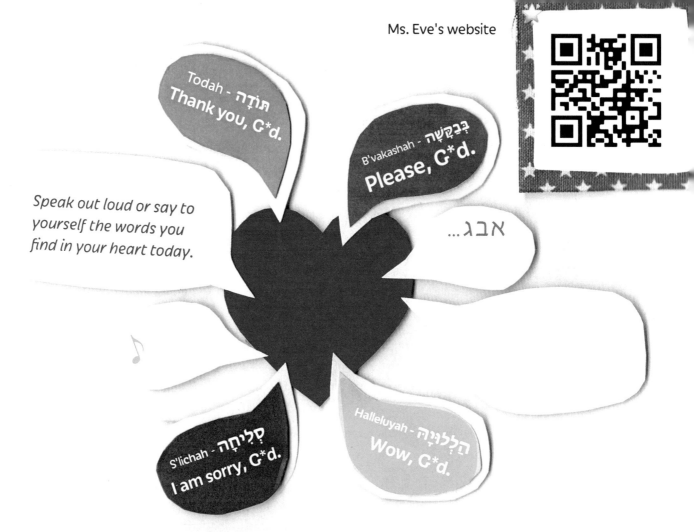

Book a "Words From My Heart" prayer experience, show, or workshop for students, parents, or educators at **www.shalomeve.com**

You can also send me your message and share the prayers you created. I'd love to hear from you!

40 ♥